Hate Crimes

CRIME, JUSTICE, AND PUNISHMENT

Hate Crimes

Laura D'Angelo

Austin Sarat, GENERAL EDITOR

CHELSEA HOUSE PUBLISHERS
Philadelphia

Frontispiece: Ku Klux Klan rally, 1991.

Chelsea House Publishers

Editor in Chief Stephen Reginald
Production Manager Pamela Loos
Art Director Sara Davis
Picture Editor Judy Hasday
Senior Production Editor Lisa Chippendale

Staff for HATE CRIMES

Senior Editor John Ziff
Associate Art Director/Designer Takeshi Takahashi
Picture Researcher Gillian Speeth
Cover Illustration Takeshi Takahashi

3 5 7 9 8 6 4

Library of Congress Cataloging-in-Publication Data

D'Angelo, Laura.
Hate crimes / Laura D'Angelo.
    p.   cm.
Includes bibliographical references and index.
Summary: Discusses the increasing incidence of crimes that
are motivated by bias against another person or group,
examining the causes and occurrences of such hate crimes
and the psychology of those who commit them.

ISBN 0-7910-4266-9 (hardcover)

1. Hate crimes—United States—Juvenile literature. 2.
Minorities—Crimes against—United States—Juvenile literature. 3. Prejudices—United States—Juvenile literature.
[1. Hate crimes. 2. Prejudices.] I. Title.
HV6250.3.U5D35 1998
364.1—dc21   97-39090
                                                        CIP
                                                        AC

Contents

Crime, Justice, and Punishment

Fears and Fascinations:

An Introduction to Crime, Justice, and Punishment

By Austin Sarat

We live with crime and images of crime all around us. Crime evokes in most of us a deep aversion, a feeling of profound vulnerability, but it also evokes an equally deep fascination. Today, in major American cities the fear of crime is a major fact of life, some would say a disproportionate response to the realities of crime. Yet the fear of crime is real, palpable in the quickened steps and furtive glances of people walking down darkened streets. At the same time, we eagerly follow crime stories on television and in movies. We watch with a "who done it" curiosity, eager to see the illicit deed done, the investigation undertaken, the miscreant brought to justice and given his just deserts. On the streets the presence of crime is a reminder of our own vulnerability and the precariousness of our taken-for-granted rights and freedoms. On television and in the movies the crime story gives us a chance to probe our own darker motives, to ask "Is there a criminal within?" as well as to feel the collective satisfaction of seeing justice done.

Fear and fascination, these two poles of our engagement with crime, are, of course, only part of the story. Crime is, after all, a major social and legal problem, not just an issue of our individual psychology. Politicians today use our fear of, and fascination with, crime for political advantage. How we respond to crime, as well as to the political uses of the crime issue, tells us a lot about who we are as a people as well as what we value and what we tolerate. Is our response compassionate or severe? Do we seek to understand or to punish, to enact an angry vengeance or to rehabilitate and welcome the criminal back into our midst? The CRIME, JUSTICE, AND PUNISHMENT series is designed to explore these themes, to ask why we are fearful and fascinated, to probe the meanings and motivations of crimes and criminals and of our responses to them, and, finally, to ask what we can learn about ourselves and the society in which we live by examining our responses to crime.

Crime is always a challenge to the prevailing normative order and a test of the values and commitments of law-abiding people. It is sometimes a Raskolnikov-like act of defiance, an assertion of the unwillingness of some to live according to the rules of conduct laid out by organized society. In this sense, crime marks the limits of the law and reminds us of law's all-too-regular failures. Yet sometimes there is more desperation than defiance in criminal acts; sometimes they signal a deep pathology or need in the criminal. To confront crime is thus also to come face-to-face with the reality of social difference, of class privilege and extreme deprivation, of race and racism, of children neglected, abandoned, or abused whose response is to enact on others what they have experienced themselves. And occasionally crime, or what is labeled a criminal act, represents a call for justice, an appeal to a higher moral order against the inadequacies of existing law.

Figuring out the meaning of crime and the motivations of criminals and whether crime arises from defiance, desperation, or the appeal for justice is never an easy task. The motivations and meanings of crime are as varied as are the persons who engage in criminal conduct. They are as mysterious as any of the mysteries of the human soul. Yet the desire to know the secrets of crime and the criminal is a strong one, for in that knowledge may lie one step on the road to protection, if not an assurance of one's own personal safety. Nonetheless, as strong as that desire may be, there is no available technology that can allow us to know the whys of crime with much confidence, let alone a scientific certainty. We can, however, capture something about crime by studying the defiance, desperation, and quest for justice that may be associated with it. Books in the CRIME, JUSTICE, AND PUNISHMENT series will take up that challenge. They tell stories of crime and criminals, some famous, most not, some glamorous and exciting, most mundane and commonplace.

This series will, in addition, take a sober look at American criminal justice, at the procedures through which we investigate crimes and identify criminals, at the institutions in which innocence or guilt is determined. In these procedures and institutions we confront the thrill of the chase as well as the challenge of protecting the rights of those who defy our laws. It is through the efficiency and dedication of law enforcement that we might capture the criminal; it is in the rare instances of their corruption or brutality that we feel perhaps our deepest betrayal. Police, prosecutors, defense lawyers, judges, and jurors administer criminal justice and in their daily actions give substance to the guarantees of the Bill of Rights. What is an adversarial system of justice? How does it work? Why do we have it? Books in the CRIME, JUSTICE, AND PUNISHMENT series will examine the thrill of the chase as we seek to capture the criminal. They will also reveal the drama and majesty of the criminal trial as well as the day-to-day reality of a criminal justice system in which trials are the exception and negotiated pleas of guilty are the rule.

When the trial is over or the plea has been entered, when we have separated the innocent from the guilty, the moment of punishment has arrived. The injunction to punish the guilty, to respond to pain inflicted by inflicting pain, is as old as civilization itself. "An eye for an eye and a tooth for a tooth" is a biblical reminder that punishment must measure pain for pain. But our response to the criminal must be better than and different from the crime itself. The biblical admonition, along with the constitutional prohibition of "cruel and unusual punishment," signals that we seek to punish justly and to be just not only in the determination of who can and should be punished, but in how we punish as well. But neither reminder tells us what to do with the wrongdoer. Do we rape the rapist, or burn the home of the arsonist? Surely justice and decency say no. But, if not, then how can and should we punish? In a world in which punishment is neither identical to the crime nor an automatic response to it, choices must be made and we must make them. Books in the CRIME, JUSTICE, AND PUNISHMENT series will examine those choices and the practices, and politics, of punishment. How do we punish and why do we punish as we do? What can we learn about the rationality and appropriateness of today's responses to crime by examining our past and its responses? What works? Is there, and can there be, a just measure of pain?

CRIME, JUSTICE, AND PUNISHMENT brings together books on some of the great themes of human social life. The books in this series capture our fear and fascination with crime and examine our responses to it. They remind us of the deadly seriousness of these subjects. They bring together themes in law, literature, and popular culture to challenge us to think again, to think anew, about subjects that go to the heart of who we are and how we can and will live together.

*   *   *   *   *

We live in a society that is characterized by both great personal freedom and great social diversity. Diversity means that all of us must find ways to live together with others who do not share our heritage, our culture, or our values. At minimum, it invites tolerance for difference; at most, diversity invites a rich and engaged pluralism in which individuals and groups are enriched by their contacts with others. But there is an underside to diversity. Ever since Tocqueville visited America at the start of the 19th century, commentators have expressed doubts about the capacity of Americans to live together harmoniously. They worried that because we are free we are able to voice prejudice, practice discrimination, express hatred. Today the challenges of living in a racially, culturally, and ethnically diverse society are again pressing on us. Debates about affirmative action, bilingual education, and multiculturalism are the latest manifestations of the dilemma of difference that Americans face.

Hate Crimes is a timely reminder of the dark possibilities in a society that is both as diverse and free as ours. Through vivid example and careful historical analysis this book shows the deep and painful ways in which prejudice has been expressed. *Hate Crimes* traces the origins of hatred to ways in which we are brought up and to the images that surround us in popular culture. It describes the psychology of hate and shows how hatred can be expressed as either an aggressive or defensive response to those unlike ourselves. This book provides a fascinating account of the ways particular political groups seek to mobilize and direct hatred and how American society has tried to combat hate crimes.

Should hate crimes be punished more severely than other crimes? Can we combat prejudice by punishing its expression? Can any of us be truly free until all of us are free from the threats posed by hate crimes? *Hate Crimes* addresses these and other questions that are among the most vexing of our age.

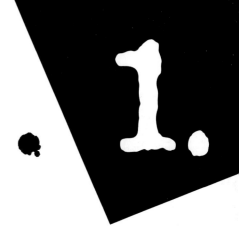

PRIDE AND PREJUDICE

Mulugeta Seraw was standing under a streetlight in front of his home, laughing with two friends who had parked their car at the curb. Seraw and his pals, Tilahun Antneh and Wondwosen Tesfaye, had just come back from a good-bye party for a man returning to their home-land, Ethiopia.

Seraw had left Ethiopia seven years earlier to escape famine and to pursue his dream of becoming an Amer-ican businessman. He had moved in with his uncle in Portland, Oregon, and begun learning English. Soon he was studying business at a local college and making ends meet by working as an airport shuttle-bus driver.

On the night of the good-bye party—November 13,

A gardener goes about his work amid the desecrated gravestones of a Jewish cemetery. What sets painting these symbols of racial hatred apart from ordinary vandalism is the intent: to intimidate an entire group of people.

1988—as the three Ethiopians were winding down their evening of merriment, three other men were capping off a night of drinking and fighting. Unbeknownst to Seraw, these men had fixed their hostile gaze on him as he stood under the streetlight. For one reason, and one reason alone, they plotted a violent confrontation with him: because he was black.

The men belonged to a group called East Side Pride, a collection of skinheads—young racists sporting shaved heads and heavy boots, who often expressed their hatred of minorities through street violence. They piled into a car and pulled up behind Seraw and his companions. Skinhead Kyle Brewster yelled out, "Move the car."

When the Ethiopians didn't respond, Brewster pulled out a gun and shouted, "Go back to your own country."

From behind the wheel of the car, one of Seraw's friends flicked on the headlights and turned the key in the ignition. But the car wouldn't start.

Brewster jumped out, poking his finger into Seraw's chest. In a matter of seconds, his two bat-wielding companions, Steve Strasser and Ken Mieske, bounded toward the startled Ethiopian.

Seraw's friends hurried out of the car to come to his defense. Tesfaye was knocked to the ground, where he was beaten and kicked repeatedly. Mieske swung a baseball bat at the car, smashing the rear window and then the taillight. Antneh managed to climb back into the car, get it started, and drive off.

But Seraw wasn't as lucky. He was surrounded by Mieske and Brewster, who pummeled him with their fists. Mieske, known as "Ken Death," lived up to his grisly nickname. He swung a bat across the back of Seraw's head three times, smashing the young man's skull. The dying Seraw let out an ear-piercing wail.

The skinheads, who had never before laid eyes on their victims and didn't know if Seraw was dead or alive, jumped into their car and fled. The bloody clash left them feeling exhilarated.

Seraw was left crumpled in a pool of blood. His friend Tesfaye dashed to his side, shaking him. "He's dead. He's dead," he cried.

Six hours after arriving at the hospital, Seraw died of fractures to his skull.

The vicious murder drew national attention to the skinheads and their violent cult of hatred. It also cast a spotlight on the rising tide of hate, or bias, crimes— crimes motivated by hostility toward a victim's race, religion, ethnic background, sexual orientation, or gender.

Whether directed at blacks, Asians, Jews, Arabs, women, or homosexuals, hate crimes have been increasing at an alarming rate. The killing of Seraw signaled a dark and growing mood of intolerance in the United States, where a national pattern of bigotry has found expression in an epidemic of shouted slurs, vandalism, and violence.

Although they may haunt victims—and, perhaps, local communities—for years, the details of most hate crimes fade quickly from the public consciousness. But a few recent acts of hate seem destined to endure as scars on the nation's psyche, troubling reminders of the fragility of toleration in our diverse society:

- In 1989 the racially motivated killing of 16-year-old Yusuf Hawkins by a bat- and gun-wielding mob of teenagers in Brooklyn showed Americans that hate doesn't have to be organized to be deadly.
- A violent clash between blacks and Jews in Crown Heights, another neighborhood in New York City, a few years later revealed that hate can explode between minority groups who live side by side.
- In 1991 the videotaped beating of black motorist Rodney King by white police officers enraged African Americans. The acquittal of the officers

Simmering racial and ethnic animosity reached a flash point in Los Angeles with the 1992 acquittal of four white police officers accused in the beating of black motorist Rodney King. Above: Looters at a South Central L.A. stereo store. Opposite page: A Korean-American shopkeeper with the AK-47 assault rifles he plans to use to defend his property from African-American looters.

involved in the beating sparked three days of riots in Los Angeles, during which blacks randomly attacked whites and lashed out at Korean-American merchants, some of whom resorted to deadly force to ward off black looters—further proof of how contagious hate can be.

Race motivates the majority of hate crimes in the United States, with blacks being the most frequently targeted group. Though it happens less often, whites, too, can be the victims of racially charged attacks.

Prejudice against religion is another impetus for many hate crimes. In the United States, Jews are targeted the most, but Jehovah's Witnesses and Muslims are also frequent victims of hate attacks.

Simmering tensions between ethnic groups also sometimes explode into acts of violence. Mexicans, Asian Americans, Indians, and Arabs have all been recent victims of hate crimes in the United States.

But hate isn't confined to race, religion, and ethnicity. Prejudice against gay men and lesbians has sparked attacks, and antigay crimes tend to be particularly brutal.

Though some people argue that women constitute the largest group of hate victims, they are seldom included in law enforcement statistics on hate crimes. States have been grappling with the question of whether violent crimes against women, especially rape and battery, should be prosecuted as crimes of bias. Some states permit such prosecutions when there is overwhelming evidence that the attacker's motivation was hatred of women; other states don't consider violence against women a category of hate crime.

The Seraw attack followed a pattern typical of a bias crime. The assailants attacked in a group. They were young, white males who chose their victims at random. They instigated the fight with threats and racial slurs.

Another hallmark of many hate crimes—savagery—was evidenced in the Seraw attack. The skinheads sought not simply to intimidate their victims or to get them to do something (ostensibly they attacked because the victims didn't move the car), but to inflict serious bodily injury or even death. They continued pummeling Seraw even after he was no longer capable of defending himself.

The term *hate crimes* denotes a range of bias-motivated criminal acts, from vandalism to murder. The legal definition, as clarified by several recent Supreme Court decisions, distinguishes between purely verbal or symbolic expressions of hatred (which are frequently called hate speech) and actual conduct. Words may be weapons, but they are protected by the Constitution. Actions are not.

It seems simple, but the line is not always so clear. Sometimes a hate crime is identified only by the speech that precedes it—as when an assault follows a series of racial slurs, for example. Complicating the situation further, state laws regarding what constitutes a hate crime—and how such crimes can be punished—vary. Some states have stand-alone laws that allow hate crimes to be prosecuted as separate offenses; others have penalty-enhancement statutes that permit the prosecution of a hate crime only in connection with another offense. And states differ in which groups their hate-crime laws protect. No federal law deals specifically with hate crimes, but a defendant may be prosecuted in federal court for violating another person's

WATCH OUT
NIGGERS
TEXAS
KLAN
IS GETTING
BIGGER

Members of the Ku Klux Klan march through Houston, July 1990.

civil rights—which, it might be argued, amounts to pretty much the same thing as prosecution for a hate crime.

If legal definitions are somewhat elusive, the crucial elements in any hate crime are the offender's motivation in selecting a victim based on that person's membership in a group and the effect the crime has on the group. Breaking a window and painting a swastika on a wall may both be acts of vandalism, for example, but the former affects only the owner of the building, whereas the latter affects any Jew who sees the graffiti. Perpetrators of hate crimes not only want to hurt the target of their crimes, they also want to intimidate or terrorize an entire community. The random selection of a victim strikes fear into the heart of everyone in the group. If anyone can be attacked, then everyone is vulnerable. Seraw's murder, for example, had a chilling effect throughout Portland's African-American community, as black people realized with frightening clarity that any of them could have been the one standing on a residential street talking with friends when the skinheads struck.

Organized hate groups, like the East Side Pride skinheads, account for only a fraction of all hate crimes. But experts say their influence can't be underestimated. Those groups set the stage for many other crimes by promoting hate and hate-inspired violence. Through literature, slogans, and rallies—and the coverage they receive on television and radio—hate groups inspire impressionable teenagers and unstable adults.

People who study hate crimes say that the perpetrators of these terrible acts are usually young, aimless people looking for a place to fit in. Insecure, isolated, and angry, they blame their own failures on minorities—who, they believe, receive unfair advantages in the competition for college slots and jobs.

Hate and insecurity are an especially explosive combination during adolescence. Teens, struggling to figure out who they are, often seek to belong to a group, especially one that shuns outsiders. Because of their youth and their eagerness to fit in, they are less equipped and less inclined to question the group's point of view. And some are willing to hurt others to gain the group's approval. Racist ideology plays an important role in promoting violence, especially among young group members. Seeing their victims as somehow less worthy—or even subhuman—makes it easier for attackers to justify their actions. Some may even think that nobody will care if a minority victim suffers.

Mieske fit the classic profile of a hate criminal. Abandoned by his mother as a child, he was living on the streets of Seattle by the time he was 16. At 19, he had a rap sheet that included convictions for cocaine

Netscape: Current News and Commentary
Back
Forward
Home
Reload
Images
Open
Print
Find
Stop
Location: http://204.181.176.4/stormfront/current.htm
What's New?
What's Cool?
Handbook
Net Search
Net Directory
Newsgroups
Current News and Commentary
It is simple reality that...
To be born WHITE is
an honor and a privilege...

Cyberhate: Hate groups have embraced the Internet as a means of spreading their message and recruiting members worldwide.

possession and for stealing meat and money from a Subway sandwich shop. While doing time for burglary in 1986, Mieske was lured into the fold of the white supremacists.

Brewster, a high school homecoming king and former drug user who had changed his ways, was more atypical. But he and Mieske found common ground in East Side Pride. Like most hate groups, the skinhead clique offered a justification for the failures these young men had experienced. And it offered them an easy scapegoat and a violent outlet for their hate.

Organized hate groups specifically try to woo young people between the ages of 14 and 25. The younger the recruit, the easier it is to train him or her to give up individual ideas and behave like a soldier in an army. The Aryan Nations—the most violent neo-Nazi group in North America—has sent recruiters into cities to pick up homeless kids and bring them back to its compound in Idaho for indoctrination and training.

Hate groups have also targeted schools for their information campaigns. For example, in 1986 the Ku Klux Klan (KKK) launched a recruiting effort near public schools in Madison County, Georgia. Members of the KKK, called Klansmen, handed out literature on school buses, held demonstrations near schools, and called out to students passing by. Angry parents convinced a court that the Klan was terrorizing their children, and the court ordered the KKK to stay 500 feet from the schools.

But hate groups haven't confined their recruiting efforts to traditional techniques like public demonstrations; they've also embraced the Internet. Through pages on the World Wide Web and postings on newsgroups, they've stepped up efforts to recruit from a worldwide audience, and their activities have become more difficult to monitor.

At the time of Seraw's murder, there was no way of tracking hate crimes in America. In fact, the label didn't even exist. In 1990 President George Bush signed a law authorizing the U.S. Department of Justice to keep track of crimes motivated by racial, religious, or sexual prejudice. The Hate Crimes Statistic Act directs police departments across the country to keep records on the number of hate crimes committed in their jurisdictions.

Civil rights groups applauded the passage of the law, saying that, for the first time, the country would be able to diagnose its problem with hate. Collecting data would help answer questions about hate crimes, such as whether a particular act was an isolated incident or part of a coordinated campaign. That information would show which groups were being targeted and whether hate was on the rise.

By all accounts, hate groups and hate crimes have experienced a swift growth over the past 10 years. The best estimates currently put hate crimes in America at between 10,000 and 40,000 a year. About 60 percent are committed by whites, and 60 percent are motivated by racial bias.

Groups that track hate crimes say these figures are low, however. They claim that more than half of all bias-motivated crimes go unreported to law enforcement, often because victims fear reprisals or lack faith in the justice system. And, critics maintain, when such crimes are reported, police and prosecutors often fail to classify them as hate crimes.

Police often have a hard time tracking down perpetrators of hate crimes. By the sheer force of numbers, hate groups offer members a shield of anonymity and protection when they attack their victims. The more people who take part in a brutal crime, the harder it is to pin the blame on any one person.

That shield was shattered in the aftermath of Seraw's murder. Fellow skinheads led police directly to Strasser, Mieske, and Brewster. Mieske pleaded guilty to murdering Seraw and was sentenced to life in prison. He said his motivation was race. Strasser and Brewster were convicted of first-degree manslaughter.

While they serve out their prison sentences—each received up to 20 years—Americans will grapple with the question of how hate can grip with such force that it drives people to kill.

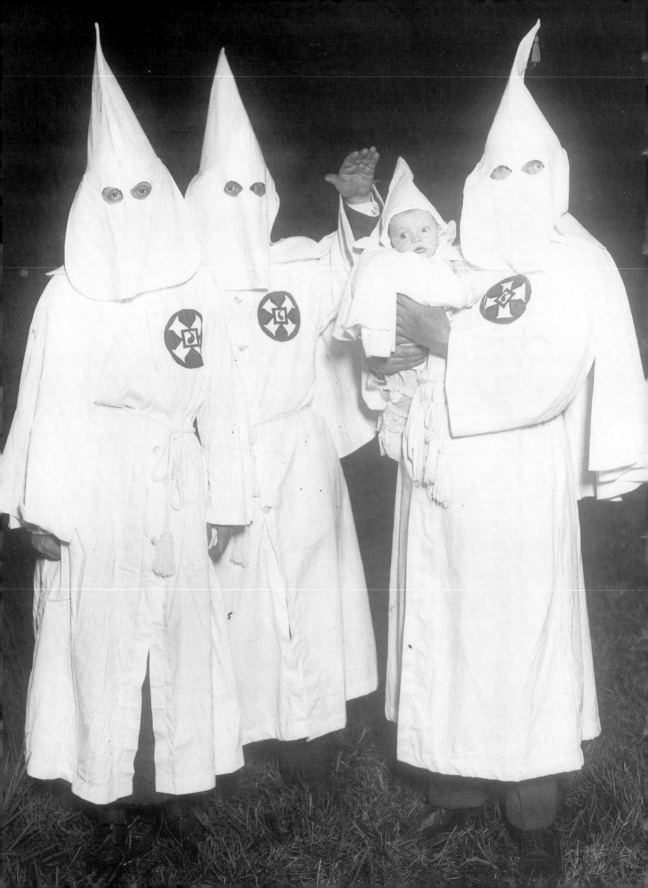

SEEDS OF HATRED

Sixteen-year-old Yusuf Hawkins and three of his friends ventured into Bensonhurst, a section of Brooklyn, on August 23, 1989, to check out a used car that had been advertised for sale in a newspaper. The black teenagers had no idea that stepping into the mostly white neighborhood would touch off a hate crime. The tragic event would leave Hawkins dead and rock an entire city already festering with racial animosity.

That day, Bensonhurst was rife with tension. Gina Feliciano, a local girl, had made it known that she had invited a group of black and Latino friends to her birthday party and that these kids were eager to fight some whites. On a hunt for the prospective guests, a mob of white kids armed themselves with baseball bats, golf clubs, and at least one gun. They cornered Hawkins and his friends. Four shots rang out. Hawkins collapsed to the ground and died.

The racial killing reverberated throughout the city.

The bigotry that fuels hate crimes is frequently learned early.

Angry black residents said the shooting was proof that many city streets were off-limits to them. Black activists and community leaders marched through Bensonhurst in protest. White residents jeered at them, hurled racial slurs, and mockingly held up watermelons.

In May 1990 a jury convicted 19-year-old Joseph Fama of Brooklyn of being the triggerman. He was sentenced to 32 years to life in prison. Two others were convicted of felony charges, two more of misdemeanors; three defendants were acquitted.

As random as the attack seemed, the seeds of racial hatred had been firmly planted in the ethnic enclave in Brooklyn. Studies later showed that racial violence occurs most often in poor or lower-middle-class white urban neighborhoods like Bensonhurst where jobs are disappearing. In their competition for jobs, the powerless turn against the powerless.

Of course, economic competition alone doesn't explain racial violence. Prejudice must also be present.

Psychologist Gordon W. Allport, author of the classic 1954 book *The Nature of Prejudice*, explained that prejudice is a feeling of dislike based on a flawed generalization of an entire group. "It may be directed toward a group as a whole, or toward an individual because he is a member of that group," Allport wrote. Prejudice might or might not ever be expressed overtly.

Prejudice is tightly woven into the fabric of our culture, but children often learn it first at home. Even parents who consider themselves open-minded may harbor biases against certain groups, sometimes without even being aware of it. And children may pick up these biases through subtle and not-so-subtle cues. For example, a parent might repeat jokes based on stereotypes; put people down because of their race, religion, or sexual orientation; or make sweeping generalizations about all members of a group.

In an interview with *New York Newsday* newspaper in 1993, Paul G. Goldenberg, the head of New Jersey's

Office of Bias Crime and Community Relations, discussed how biased attitudes take hold early in family life. The former undercover police officer said talking to children in grade school was a real eye-opener.

"I ask them, 'How many of you have heard in your own home or from your family a joke about another person or about another group or about someone because they're gay?' Normally, 100 percent of the hands in the class go up. Most of the kids are getting this message right from their own homes," he said.

Displays of prejudice go well beyond subtle signs and well beyond the family, however. According to hate-crime experts Jack Levin and Jack McDevitt, we live in a society where hatred is hip. In their book *Hate Crimes: The Rising Tide of Bigotry and Bloodshed*, the authors write:

> [W]e are in the midst of a growing culture of hate; from humor and music to religion and politics, a person's group affiliation—the fact that he or she differs from people in the in-group—is being used more and more to provide a basis for dehumanizing and insulting that person.

Radio shock jock Howard Stern. According to some hate-crime experts, entertainers who make fun of society's most powerless groups help create a climate in which prejudice is viewed as acceptable.

Levin and McDevitt point to the popularity of openly racist entertainers like the rock group Guns N' Roses and to the fiercely women-hating lyrics of some heavy metal and rap music. Stand-up comedians and radio shock jocks who verbally attack the most powerless groups of people add fuel to the fire. Their words are more than insensitive; they send an unmistakable message that making fun of certain groups is acceptable.

Not all prejudice turns into violence, but all hate crimes are an outgrowth of prejudice. What releases the brakes between feeling and acting hateful?

Allport observed that violent outbursts of hate usually follow a particular pattern. First, over an extended period of time, attackers come to blame people in the victimized group for all sorts of difficulties; often they even stop thinking of them as human. Second, there is an outside strain, such as hard economic times or fear of unemployment. Finally, some incident involving the victimized group—perhaps simply a minor provocation or even an imagined slight—occurs and sparks the attack. For example, the murder in Bensonhurst was spurred by a rumor that black teens were gearing up to fight the white kids in the neighborhood. Mulugeta Seraw was killed by skinheads who were angered that the Ethiopians had parked their car in the street.

Hate crimes tend to soar in hard economic times. During the recessions of the late 1970s and the early 1990s, bias-motivated crimes rose sharply. When jobs are scarce and money is tight, competition becomes fierce. Workers worry that they'll lose their shrinking piece of the financial pie. Scared and angry, they may look for others they can blame for their problems.

Hate crimes also tend to rise when minority groups suddenly become more visible and vocal in their demands. For example, in the 1950s, black people who began demanding their civil rights became targets of lynchings and bombings. And in recent years, high-profile issues involving gays and lesbians have captured the attention of the media and raised the ire of gay bashers. The campaign for AIDS awareness, the debate about whether gays should be allowed in the military, and the subject of same-sex marriages propelled gays and lesbians into the national spotlight. As the debate became increasingly nasty, the climate for gays and lesbians became more hostile. A report issued by the National Gay and Lesbian Task Force in 1995 showed that hate crimes against gays and lesbians skyrocketed between 1989 and 1994. Task force spokesman Robert

Bray said, "The gay community is under siege in this country. We are fighting an epidemic of violence."

A similar phenomenon was at work during the Persian Gulf War. In August 1990 Iraq invaded neighboring Kuwait, and American troops were rushed to defend another Persian Gulf nation and key American ally, Saudi Arabia. Early in 1991 the United States and its coalition of allies launched a war to expel Iraq from Kuwait. These events kicked up virulent anti-Arab sentiment and set off a rash of hate crimes against Arab Americans, who became targets of harassing phone calls, death threats, and beatings. As with other outbreaks of hate crimes, a strong element of irrationality accompanied the victimizations: Iraq is an Arab nation, but so are Kuwait and Saudi Arabia, the nations the United States was defending.

Two gay men at a rally for homosexual rights. Experts have observed that hate crimes against minority groups tend to proliferate when those groups become more visible or vocal in their demands. This was the case with gays and lesbians in the first half of the 1990s, when gays in the military and same-sex marriages were prominent and controversial issues.

HATE STRIKES

The murder of Mulugeta Seraw became a searing symbol of racial hatred, but statistics show that only a small percentage of hate crimes are committed by skinheads, the Klan, the Aryan Nations, and other organized hate groups. The killing of Yusuf Hawkins was more typical—carried out by seemingly normal, boy-next-door types who didn't sport shaved heads or hooded robes.

According to hate-crime experts Jack Levin and Jack McDevitt, the largest percentage of hate crimes are committed by young white men—in their teens or early twenties—who are looking for excitement. These so-called thrill seekers don't belong to a group. Their

Mourners carry the coffin of Michael Griffith, a 23-year-old black man who was hit by a car and killed after a mob of white youths chased him onto a busy highway. Armed with baseball bats and tree branches, the mob attacked Griffith and his two companions when their car broke down in the whites' neighborhood, the Howard Beach section of Queens.

crimes are spontaneous acts, born of rage. After guzzling alcohol with their buddies, for example, they look for someone to beat up or some property to destroy. They may deface a synagogue or turn over gravestones. Or they may get their thrills by watching a defenseless victim suffer. Thrill seekers pick blacks or gays or other minorities as targets in part because they believe society won't care if these people are victimized.

A second type of hate crime is committed by assailants who believe they are defending their turf against outsiders. They may attack anyone perceived to pose a threat to themselves, their property, their jobs, or their neighborhood. Turf defenders typically live in homogeneous enclaves, and often they construe the mere presence in their neighborhood of someone of, for example, a different race as a threat and a call to action. In Bensonhurst a mob of whites participated in the killing of Hawkins simply because he was black and had ventured into their neighborhood.

Instead of assaulting their victims, some turf defenders resort to acts of hate speech to terrorize them. A black family who has moved into an all-white neighborhood, for example, may be greeted by a burning cross on their lawn. The intent, of course, is to send a threatening message to that family—and to any other black family who might consider taking up residence in the neighborhood.

Despite their deep-seated prejudices, turf defenders, unlike thrill seekers, don't look for victims; their hatred manifests itself only when an outsider appears in what they've defined as their territory. That distinguishes them also from the third and rarest group of hate criminals: mission criminals, so called because they believe it is their mission to rid the world of an entire class of people. The assailant in a mission hate crime almost always acts alone, and the crime typically takes the form of a bloody rampage in a public place, since the goal is to kill as many members of the hated group as

possible. According to Levin and McDevitt, the perpetrators of mission crimes suffer from psychosis, mental illness that puts them completely out of touch with reality.

Gays and lesbians are the most frequently targeted victims of thrill-seeking hate criminals, according to Levin and McDevitt. The attackers are often teenagers with an irrational fear and hatred of homosexuals.

One of the most atrocious homophobic crimes in recent memory occurred in 1990. Julio Rivera, a gay man from the South Bronx, was returning home from work at 2 A.M. when three young men—Erik Brown, 21; Esat Bici, 19; and Daniel Doyle, 21—lured him into an isolated corner of a school yard. There, they repeatedly smashed him on the head with a hammer and beat

Nine of the 12 youths charged in the Howard Beach case leave the Queens Criminal Court Building, February 11, 1987. In the taxonomy of hate criminals, these youths would be classified as turf defenders: the presence of "outsiders" in their neighborhood triggered their violent behavior.

him on the head and face with a pipe wrench and beer bottle. Doyle struck the fatal blow, plunging a knife into Rivera's back.

Clinging to life, Rivera managed to stagger from the school yard. When his friend Alan Sack arrived at the scene, he found Rivera covered in blood and lying on the sidewalk. Sack pleaded, "Hang on, you're going to make it! I swear you're going to make it!"

But Rivera did not hang on for long. He was declared dead a few hours later in a nearby hospital. The murder mobilized gay-rights groups, who saw the slaying as symptomatic of the rising tide of violence against gays and lesbians. When no arrests were made and the New York City Police Department refused to categorize the crime as a bias incident, gay-rights groups mounted considerable pressure, staging angry demonstrations. Four months after Rivera was murdered, police arrested the assailants. Nine months after the attack, the police labeled the case a crime inspired by bias.

The leader of the three attackers, Daniel Doyle, admitted that he and his friends had been drinking beer at a skinhead party on the night of the slaying. As the party drew to a close, Doyle suggested that they find someone to beat up. They headed to a popular gay cruising area in Jackson Heights, Queens, to find a likely victim. Doyle said they had killed Rivera because he was gay.

During the trial, Doyle appeared as the prosecution's star witness. He had been allowed to plead to a reduced charge of manslaughter in return for testifying against his two friends.

Unlike most hate-inspired gay and lesbian killings, the murder of Rivera resulted in arrests and convictions. Doyle was sentenced to $8^1/3$ to 25 years in prison. Brown and Bici were each sentenced to prison terms of 25 years to life for their role in the slaying.

Rivera's murderers had invaded a well-known gay

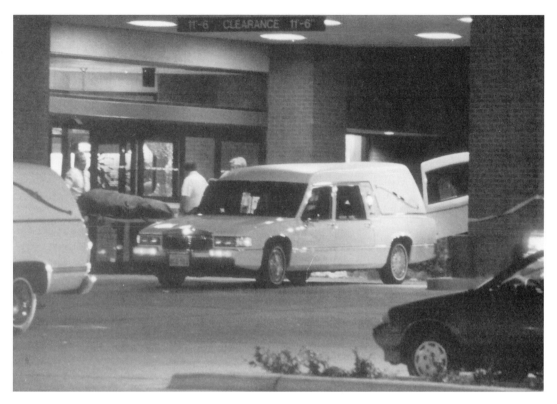

hangout to hunt down a victim. But attackers who believe they are protecting their turf from outsiders usually find their victims in their own backyards. Like the thrill seekers, these criminals generally don't belong to organized hate groups.

In the famous hate crime that would become known by the name of the neighborhood where it occurred, Howard Beach, another mob of white youths showed America how deadly prejudice can be.

On the wintry night of December 20, 1986, a tan Buick Regal carrying three black men—Michael Griffith, 23; Cedric Sandiford, 36; and Timothy Grimes, 19—broke down on Cross Bay Boulevard in a section of eastern Queens, a predominantly white part of that borough in New York City.

The men got out of the car and began walking. The very presence of these "outsiders" in the mostly white

Twenty-three hearses stopped at Luby's Cafeteria in Killeen, Texas, after George Hennard authored one of the deadliest hate crimes in U.S. history there. Apparently motivated by a hatred of women, Hennard crashed his pickup truck through the restaurant's plate-glass window and proceeded to open fire on patrons and employees with two semiautomatic pistols before killing himself.

Acting as his own attorney, Colin Ferguson makes a point during his trial for the 1993 shooting spree on a Long Island commuter train that left 6 dead and 19 wounded. As with other so-called mission hate crimes, mental illness played a role in Ferguson's deadly rampage.

neighborhood of Howard Beach was seen as a threat by a gang of youths who lived there.

As the black men approached a local pizzeria, a car coming at them slammed to a halt. Inside the car were Jon Lester, a 17-year-old gangster wanna-be, and three friends. The two groups exchanged harsh words, some of them racial. The whites threatened to return. The blacks said they'd be waiting.

Lester and his companions burst into a basement beer party. "There's niggers on the boulevard! Let's go kill them!" he shouted.

Armed with baseball bats and tree branches, Lester and his friends piled into several cars and headed back to the pizzeria. They cornered the three black men, who ran after more cars arrived.

The armed mob chased Griffith for eight blocks. In a desperate attempt to escape, he ran onto the busy Belt Parkway and was struck and killed by a car.

During the trial, the prosecution maintained that Lester had been part of the mob that had chased Griffith onto the Belt Parkway. Then, after seeing Griffith struck down by the car, the prosecution said, Lester had turned around to go after Sandiford, who had been beaten bloody with bats and sticks. A gaping wound to his head would require 66 stitches to close.

At the trial, Sandiford pointed his finger at Lester and told the jury he had pleaded with his attackers, "Please, oh God, don't kill me. I have a son like you."

Grimes had managed to jump over a wall and escape.

Nine people were convicted for their roles in the attack. Three were convicted of manslaughter and assault. Six others were convicted of lesser charges and were sentenced to community service or, in one case, six months in jail.

In a mission hate crime, the assailant is usually a loner, not part of a band of drunken hunters or a member of an organized group. Through the distorted lens of mental illness, he sees himself as being put on the earth to eliminate an entire group of people. Two of the deadliest mission hate crimes were rampages against women. In both cases the perpetrators ended their sprees by turning their guns on themselves.

Marc Lepine's hatred of women had been simmering ever since an engineering school had turned down his application. A 25-year-old college dropout who had aspirations of becoming an engineer, Lepine was furious that he couldn't get into engineering school and several women had.

Eventually his rage turned murderous. Gripping a semiautomatic assault rifle, Lepine walked into the

University of Montreal's Ecole Polytechnique in Canada. It was 5 P.M. on December 6, 1989, and the school twinkled with Christmas decorations. Lepine stalked the six-floor building, roaming the cafeteria, hallways, and classrooms and shooting at women. He marched into one class, ordered the men and women to separate, and then told the men to leave. As the women watched in mute terror, Lepine announced, "You're all a bunch of feminists. I hate feminists." He then opened fire on the group.

In the worse mass murder Canada had ever seen, Lepine killed 14 people in cold blood, all of them women. He wounded nine more women and four men before shooting himself. Police found a suicide note on his body in which Lepine blamed feminists for ruining his life.

Rage against women led to one of the largest mass murders in the United States as well. George Hennard not only blamed women for his problems but also believed they were responsible for the problems of the world. In October 1991 Hennard, 35, crashed his pickup truck through the window of a restaurant in Killeen, Texas. He pulled two semiautomatic pistols on patrons and employees, fatally shooting 23 people and injuring 22 others. Fifteen of the dead were women. Witnesses heard him say, "Wait till those . . . women in Belton see this! I wonder if they'll think it was worth it."

Police quickly closed in on him, but not in time to make a capture. Hennard put a gun to his head and took his own life. Investigators never established what kind of real or imagined problems Hennard had had with women.

Most hate crimes are perpetrated by white men, but blacks and Latinos also commit acts of hate. Sometimes hate crimes are easy to spot, but other times the motivation isn't so clear.

In some mission-type crimes it's hard to say whether the driving force is hate or mental instability. That's the question that dogged Americans in 1993 when Colin Ferguson, a 36-year-old black man, gunned down passengers in a crowded commuter train on Long Island, New York. Six people died and 19 were wounded in the rush-hour attack.

Police found handwritten notes that Ferguson, a native of Jamaica, was carrying. In them, he detailed his hatred for whites, Asians, and "Uncle Tom blacks." Police labeled the shooting a bias crime.

Ferguson's first team of lawyers wanted to mount an insanity defense. They intended to claim that Ferguson had been driven crazy by years of exposure to white racism and bigotry, which, they would assert, he had endured after moving to the United States. The lawyers referred to the condition as "black rage." But Ferguson refused to agree to an insanity plea, and he turned down representation from those lawyers. Instead, he acted as his own attorney and launched a bizarre defense. In an often rambling presentation to the jury, he claimed to be innocent of the charges against him. He said he'd been set up, maintaining that he had fallen asleep and a white man had stolen his gun from a bag under his seat.

That story was ripped to shreds as the survivors of the massacre, one by one, took the stand and identified Ferguson as the triggerman.

Though he was convicted of murder, Ferguson was acquitted of 25 counts of civil rights violations stemming from the charge that the shootings were motivated by racial bias. The jurors said that they didn't find him guilty of the civil rights charges because his victims were whites, blacks, Asians, and Latinos. He hated all of them.

Hate is an emotion as old and powerful as love. And the roots of America's epidemic of hate crimes can be traced back to its most violent confrontation on race: the Civil War.

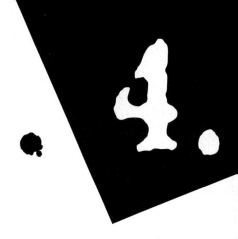

THE INVISIBLE
EMPIRE

In 1866 six young ex-soldiers were sitting around a house looking for something to do. They had just returned from the Civil War, this nation's bloodiest conflict, where they had fought for the Confederacy.

Compared to the excitement and exhilaration they had experienced during the war, they found life in their hometown, Pulaski, Tennessee, boring. So they decided to form a social club just for kicks. The group would be built around practical jokes and outrageous rituals. One soldier, John Kennedy, suggested naming the group "Kuklux" after the Greek word for circle. The friends agreed to pair the word with "Klan," since they were all of Scottish descent. Ku Klux Klan sounded just the right note: mysterious and silly.

The ex-soldiers raided the linen closet and draped themselves in sheets and pillowcases. Then they paraded through town, delighting in the chuckles that their ridiculous costumes evoked from onlookers.

The spectacle punctured the dreary mood that had descended on their town and, for that matter, on the entire South. More than a quarter million Confederate soldiers had perished during the war, and a far greater number had been wounded, leaving few families untouched by grief. Many of the South's cities had been destroyed, and the region's economy was in shambles.

And there was an immense psychological toll as well. All the death and destruction had been in vain: Southerners had fought to uphold the institution of slavery and to form an independent nation, but they had lost. Approximately 3.5 million slaves, the backbone of the South's agricultural economy, had been freed, and not only weren't the Confederate states an independent nation, but they also enjoyed less autonomy now than before the war. The U.S. Congress had dissolved the state governments, replacing them with military occupation forces and stipulating conditions that the states had to meet before they would be fully readmitted into the Union. This process of rebuilding and reintegrating the Southern states was called Reconstruction, and Southerners largely viewed it as a Northern attempt to finish the job of destroying their way of life.

Against this strained backdrop, the Ku Klux Klan was comic relief. The ex-soldiers started to make their costumes more elaborate by incorporating spooky occult symbols such as skeletons and half-moons.

Young men who heard about the troupe of jokesters were eager to join. When someone expressed an interest in signing up, the band of revelers would pay him a surprise visit at night. After blindfolding the prospective member, they'd escort him to a field for a hazing ritual. Men in other counties began asking the original founders if they could establish their own chapters of the KKK.

Soon, the hijinks took a terrifying turn. The Klansmen, bored with hazing their white peers, turned to

blacks as a source of amusement. They would visit the homes of black families, claiming to be ghosts of Confederate soldiers looking for revenge. The Klansmen delighted in exaggerating the reactions of blacks, whom they described as terrified by the ghosts. The stories, which tapped into a racial stereotype that blacks were gullible, spurred on night raids that became increasingly threatening. The former slaves were frightened not by the possibility of seeing a ghost, but by the reality of being targeted by the night riders.

All vestiges of fun quickly evaporated. The night visits were no longer insensitive pranks but bona fide acts of racial terror, and the Klan began to take shape as one of the most feared organizations in America. During an organizational meeting in 1867, the Pulaski

Freed slaves in a Southern town shortly after the Civil War. Resentment of blacks' new status—along with lingering bitterness over the war and economic hardship—made many white Southerners sympathetic to the Klan's goals.

Nathan Bedford Forrest, who had been one of the Confederacy's ablest generals, took command of the Ku Klux Klan in 1867. Within a few years, Forrest had molded the Klan into a vigilante army opposed to Reconstruction.

den passed an oath of secrecy and created passwords and secret handshakes.

That same year, Nathan Bedford Forrest took command of the Klan, assuming the title of "Imperial Wizard." Forrest, who had been one of the Confederacy's most brilliant generals, gave the group a military structure. He turned the Klan into a vigilante army opposed to Reconstruction. The group's political agenda was fairly simple: keeping blacks from voting and reclaiming white supremacy.

Under Forrest's reign, the Klan experienced spectacular growth. Forrest traveled throughout the South, recruiting leaders in different states. By 1868 the KKK boasted among its ranks newspaper editors, judges, political leaders, and even ministers.

The Klan became known as the Invisible Empire, but it was actually becoming more and more visible. Meetings were announced in newspapers alongside flattering stories about the group; parades drummed up further support. At one point Forrest estimated that there were 550,000 Klansmen throughout the country—40,000 in Tennessee alone.

Most white Southerners were sympathetic to the Klan's goals, though many disapproved of the group's tactics. Others who opposed the Klan were afraid to speak out against it.

In 1868 the Klan embarked on a reign of terror in Tennessee that lasted three years. Using the tools of slavery—whippings and lynchings—Klansmen terrorized and murdered blacks. They burned down schools that admitted black pupils and attacked their white teachers, as well as any whites they viewed as sympathetic to Reconstruction. Throughout the South, hundreds of blacks fearing for their lives left their homes at night to sleep in the woods, where they would be safe from the night-prowling Klansmen.

When a public backlash against its activities prompted many respected members of the community to drop out of the Klan, the group stanched its losses by using on whites the tactics it employed to terrorize blacks. The Klan not only began intimidating men into joining, but it also threatened those who tried to leave.

As the Klan continued to grow, it became increasingly unwieldy. Unable to control the organization in the military manner to which he was accustomed, Forrest bowed out and ordered the Klan to disband. But it was too late. The Klan was armed and dangerous and thriving on the force of Forrest's momentum. The acts of brutality continued until people called on Congress to intervene.

In 1871 lawmakers passed the Ku Klux Act, giving

Hooded Klansmen rout black soldiers in a scene from D. W. Griffith's 1915 film The Birth of a Nation. *The motion picture spurred widespread sympathy for—and boosted membership in—the KKK.*

the president authority to use troops and suspend civil rights to quash disturbances in the defeated South. That year President Ulysses S. Grant ordered federal troops into South Carolina to combat the rising tide of Klan violence. There and elsewhere, military investigations produced hundreds of arrests, and trials were held in federal courts. Many Klan leaders fled, and the organization dissolved.

But the Klan had declared a victory. Through force and intimidation it had succeeded in keeping blacks away from the voting polls and out of white schools, restaurants, and other public places. Many Southern Klan sympathizers had gained political power, and this political base would help keep intact the system of segregation well into the next century.

Four and a half decades later, in the midst of World War I, the KKK rose again. Its revival was boosted by D. W. Griffith's film *The Birth of a Nation*, which romanticized the history of the Klan. The movie depicted the hooded night riders as valiant heroes and the newly freed slaves as evil savages. Based on a 1905 novel, *The Clansman*, by Thomas Dixon, the film played in 1915 to packed movie houses throughout the country. It was even privately viewed and praised by President Woodrow Wilson.

Suddenly, the Klan had piqued the curiosity and captured the sympathy of the American white mainstream. And Imperial Wizard William Joseph Simmons used the opportunity to revive the dying group in a ceremony on top of Georgia's Stone Mountain in 1915. Behind him burned a fiery cross, a symbol he popularized after picking it up from his reading of *The Clansman*.

In the years that followed, Simmons brought his skills as a former minister to the Klan's top post. He recruited Protestant leaders by modeling Klan ceremonies on church rituals and condemning the "immoralities" of the Roaring Twenties, like jazz and bootlegging. Though it was the first time the Klan had adopted a spiritual component, the group also broadened its list of hated enemies to include Catholics and Jews. The Klan's new message—a nostalgia for simpler times and suspicion of immigrants, who had been arriving on America's shores in large numbers—had broad-based appeal. By the mid-1920s, the Invisible Empire boasted a membership of three to four million.

Klansmen conquered new territory: politics. The Klan had a hand in electing public officials and didn't shy away from flexing its political muscle. In 1924 President Calvin Coolidge signed a Klan-backed bill placing strict quotas on immigration.

The measure strongly favored white Anglo-Saxon Protestants and penalized all others. The next year Klan membership reached its peak, topping four million.

To many Americans the KKK's gains were a cause for concern. Blacks decided that they needed to organize in order to fight the Klan's influence. Groups such as the National Association for the Advancement of Colored People (NAACP) staged protests of *The Birth of a Nation*. Other predominantly white organizations, including the American Federation of Labor and the American Legion, came out publicly against the Klan.

In addition, several newspapers won Pulitzer Prizes for their exposés of Klan terror. The articles stirred so much public outrage that some states passed laws making it illegal to wear masks—legislation that was clearly aimed at the hooded terrorists. In 1925 the so-called Monkey Trial, in which Tennessee schoolteacher John Scopes was tried for teaching Darwinism, turned many Americans against the Klan's allies in certain Fundamentalist churches.

But the biggest blow to the Klan came when, also in 1925, Steve Stephenson, the Grand Dragon (statewide leader) of the KKK in Indiana, was convicted of the sordid rape and murder of a young woman whom he had abducted and literally chewed apart. The nation was shocked at the brutality of his crime. But Stephenson was even more shocked when he was sentenced to jail. He had thought his friends in law enforcement and government would pull strings to have the charges against him dropped. As he sat in prison waiting for a pardon that would never come, Stephenson's disbelief turned to outrage. The disgraced Grand Dragon decided to drop the dime on the corrupt officeholders who

had made him promises. His revelations shed new light on how Southern politicians worked hand in hand with the KKK. By the end of the decade, Klan membership had dropped to 45,000, and it continued to decline throughout the 1940s.

The civil rights movement of the 1950s set the stage for the Klan's most violent comeback. As blacks mobilized and demanded equal rights, the Klan grew determined to hobble their march toward freedom.

The move to integrate white schools and white housing complexes was seen by many southerners as another threat to their way of life. Politicians and many northerners also were opposed to integration. In 1956 the Klan galvanized. At Stone Mountain, Georgia, 3,000 Klan members pledged their commitment to

Freedom Riders rest beside the burned-out hulk of a bus near Anniston, Alabama, May 14, 1961. A mob of white segregationists had slashed the tires, set the bus on fire, and attacked the passengers as they got off. This and other widely publicized incidents of racial violence helped turn the tide of public opinion against the Klan during the 1960s.

destroying the civil rights movement. Soon thousands more had joined the fight.

Further growth in Klan membership was fueled by the 1960 election of John F. Kennedy as president and the rise of civil rights leader Martin Luther King Jr. Kennedy made the Klan's enemies list by virtue of being Catholic and sympathetic to the civil rights movement. Ten months into his presidency, the Klan's membership had reached approximately 20,000.

But the Klan had underestimated the momentum of the civil rights movement and the power of the yearning for equality felt by black Americans. The Supreme Court had already started tearing down the South's entrenched system of segregation by ordering all-white institutions to admit blacks.

In desperation the Klan embarked on a killing spree, shooting and lynching blacks and outspoken opponents. Klansmen used cross burnings to intimidate blacks and attacked nonviolent protestors. They bombed blacks' homes, the offices of civil rights workers, and black churches.

This time, however, television cameras were on the scene to document the brutality and deliver the horrific images to millions of American households.

In 1961 buses filled with white and black students headed to Alabama to challenge segregation in bus stations. The so-called Freedom Riders were met by a throng of white segregationists in Anniston, Alabama, who bombed some of the buses. In Birmingham, Alabama, a vicious mob led by the Klan beat the Freedom Riders with clubs and pipes. It was later revealed that the Birmingham police had given Klansmen a 15-minute grace period to attack the protestors.

U.S. attorney general Robert Kennedy responded by dispatching 500 federal marshals to Alabama and seeking an injunction against the Klan.

Other incidents of terror turned the tide of public opinion against the KKK. Klansmen participated in a

Imperial Wizard David Duke speaks at a 1976 press conference. By toning down the Klan's vitriolic rhetoric, Duke attempted to give the organization mainstream appeal. But, critics charged, his decrying of welfare cheats, affirmative action, and rising crime rates contained an unmistakable undercurrent of racism.

riot that resulted when James Meredith became the first black student to enroll at the University of Mississippi in Oxford in 1962. Rocks were hurled and guns fired in the melee. Klansmen were also implicated in the 1963 bombing of the Sixteenth Street Baptist Church in Birmingham, an attack that killed four black girls.

Then the Klan was suspected in the disappearance of three civil rights workers—two white and one black—in Philadelphia, Mississippi. Fed up with the Klan's arrogance, FBI director J. Edgar Hoover sent 153 agents into Neshoba County, where Philadelphia is located. The agents uncovered evidence that the local police had worked in collusion with the Klan, leading to the deaths of the young civil rights workers. The police had picked them up for speeding, then released them into the clutches of the Klan. The incident politicized students on college campuses everywhere and sparked race riots in Harlem and other northern cities. Disgust at Klan terrorism also spurred the passage of the Civil Rights Act, which was signed into law in 1964 by President Lyndon Johnson.

On March 25, 1965, Klansmen shot and killed a white civil rights volunteer, Viola Liuzzo, who was working for the Alabama Freedom March, as she drove with a black teenager in her car. Two separate juries failed to convict her three killers, who later became local heroes.

But there were other ramifications. That year Congress passed the Voting Rights Act, which removed the barriers that southern officials had used to prevent blacks from voting and also enabled African Americans to hold political office. Later in 1965, Liuzzo's killers were tried again—this time in federal court—convicted, and sentenced to 10 years in prison for violating Liuzzo's civil rights.

By 1967 the Klan's numbers had again diminished. But this time the waning Klan could not declare victory. The group's use of violence to stymie the civil rights movement had backfired. Horror at KKK tactics had mobilized public support for the Civil Rights Act of 1964 and the Voting Rights Act of 1965.

The Klan's next revival came in the mid-1970s. By then the group had polished its image under the leadership of David Duke, the smooth-talking golden boy from Louisiana who tried to transform the Klan into a mainstream organization. The Klan dropped its opposition to Catholics and toned down its racist message. Duke appealed to whites who resented special programs for minorities, such as affirmative action, which he said hurt whites. Critics frequently observed that while he avoided blatantly racist statements, Duke spoke in code, lashing out against welfare cheats and decrying rising crime rates—references that in many people's minds conjured up images of lazy and dangerous African Americans.

In 1988 the former KKK Imperial Wizard took his watered-down racism into the arena of national politics. Duke was nominated for president by the Populist Party, and though he never figured in the outcome of the election, which was won by George Bush, he managed to raise significant sums of money by bringing the fringe into the mainstream. Issues that white-supremacist groups embraced, such as opposition to affirmative action, welfare, and immigration, also appealed to numerous conservative citizens.

Today the Ku Klux Klan is no longer a united organization but rather 30 or 40 groups with different strategies and goals that continue to share the Klan name. Although the Klan continues to weaken, it hasn't disappeared. It serves as an anchor for other racist groups, including neo-Nazis, skinheads, and other organizations known loosely as patriot groups, which have grown in strength and numbers.

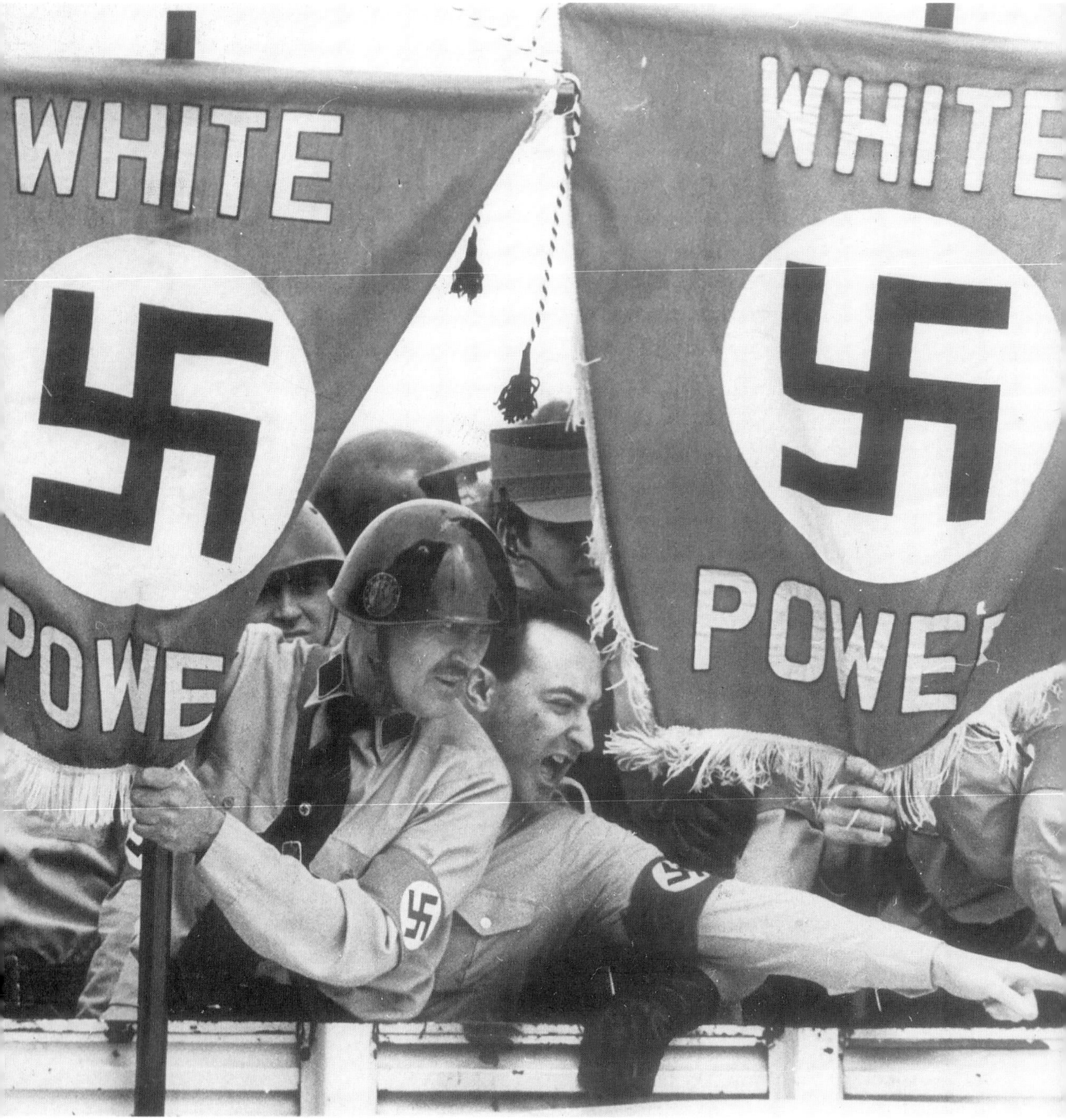
WHITE
POWE
WHITE
POWE

ORGANIZED HATE

They go by different names and salute different leaders, but hate groups of all stripes are united by a thirst for violence that's born of racial and religious intolerance.

Many of the names sound familiar: Ku Klux Klan, Christian Identity, Aryan Nations, skinheads, neo-Nazis, White Aryan Resistance. Bound by a common philosophy, these groups often overlap and join forces. More-established groups of haters, like the Klan, have worked hand in hand with the newcomers, like the skinheads. Today, former leaders of major hate groups can even be found in the extreme wings of the growing number of militias.

Hate has swept into almost every state in the country. In 1994 Klanwatch, an antihate organization, counted 277 hate groups in America. The eastern part of the country is a hotbed of white-supremacist activity, with Pennsylvania leading the way. Home to Philadelphia, the City of Brotherly Love, Pennsylvania is also

From aboard a flatbed truck, members of the Nazi Party of America react to jeers from anti-Nazi protestors lining the streets of their parade route through St. Louis, Missouri. Estimates put the number of organized hate groups in the United States at more than 275.

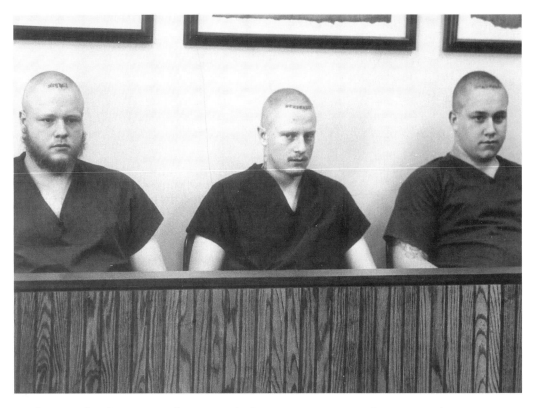

Brothers David and Bryan Freeman, along with their cousin Nelson Birdwell III, at a hearing. The three skinheads, believers in the racist Christian Identity "religion," murdered the Freemans' parents and younger brother, whom they apparently considered "race traitors."

home to 64 hate groups, more than any other state.

Though some people dismiss hate groups as a refuge for lunatics on the fringe of society, hundreds of impressionable young people join those groups every year. Sometimes the most unlikely candidates find themselves at home in a hate group.

David and Bryan Freeman were once devout Jehovah's Witnesses. A talented public speaker, Bryan, the elder of the two brothers, would address the entire religious congregation to which his family belonged. He and his brother dressed in suits and ties for school, where they showed considerable academic promise.

But the Freeman brothers turned their backs on the spiritual teachings that had played such an important role in their lives. They joined the Christian Identity, a chapter of the largest racist group in the United States, the Aryan Nations.

Though it claims to be a religion, Christian Identity is a ministry of virulent racism and anti-Semitism. Believers say that white Europeans are God's chosen people and Jews are children of Satan. Christian Identity teaches that all others are subhuman "mud people." Followers are taught to prepare for a racial holy war. They are told that anyone who opposes white supremacy is a traitor who must be destroyed.

Christian Identity energized the racist movement by introducing a religious base for hate. The Identity concepts are far-reaching; members of other hate groups are well versed in the core Identity beliefs, including the tenet that nonwhites are somehow nonhuman.

In 1993 the Freemans began attending Christian Identity meetings on a 24-acre compound near their home in Allentown, Pennsylvania. Sometimes they were joined by as many as 300 other skinheads and members of the Aryan Nations, according to Klanwatch.

Two years after joining the Christian Identity group, the Freeman brothers jettisoned their once-proper appearance and adopted a menacing front. They shaved their heads and wore engineer boots, black jeans, and T-shirts bearing the message "Eternal Hatred." They talked to their classmates about Satanism and their hatred for blacks and Jews. Problems with drugs and alcohol became part of the troubling picture.

One day Bryan, 17, showed up at school with a tattoo on his neck. It was a swastika made from human bones. On his forehead was tattooed the word *Berzerker*. (In ancient Scandinavia, a berserker was a frenzied warrior invincible in battle.) David, 16, had the German phrase *Sieg Heil* (used in Nazi Germany as a salute to Adolf Hitler) etched on his forehead.

Trouble had been brewing in the Freeman household. The boys' mother had reported that David called her a "race traitor" and warned, "I am going to kill you," according to the 1995 Klanwatch Intelligence Report, which quoted a source close to the Freeman family.

The dramatic change in the boys frightened their mother, Brenda, and their father, Dennis. In an attempt to curb their sons' neo-Nazi leanings, they threw out the hate literature kept by the teens and sold the car that the boys used to travel to Michigan for meetings with fellow skinheads.

Five days later—on February 26, 1995—Dennis and Brenda Freeman were dead. They had been bludgeoned with a baseball bat and pick handle and stabbed in the family home. Their 11-year-old son, Erik, was found stabbed to death in his bed. The brothers and their cousin, 18-year-old Nelson Birdwell III, were arrested for murder.

Christian Identity minister Mark Thomas denied teaching a philosophy of hate. He told newspaper reporters that he didn't know the Freeman brothers and had seen them only once, at a bonfire he had hosted at the group's compound.

The triple slayings brought intense scrutiny onto the Aryan Nations and the Christian Identity. The nagging question remains: Did the brothers act under the influence of the group's racist teachings?

The Freeman brothers wouldn't say. Bryan Freeman pleaded guilty to murdering his mother, and David pleaded guilty to killing his father. Both were sentenced to life in prison without parole. When Lehigh County judge Lawrence Brenner asked David why he had killed his father, Freeman responded, "I don't know."

Birdwell, also a neo-Nazi, claimed he had just watched as his two cousins killed their parents. But he was convicted in the death of his uncle, Dennis Freeman, a speck of whose blood was found on Birdwell's T-shirt. No one was convicted in Erik Freeman's death.

Like many young bigots, the Freemans and Birdwell borrowed symbols and ideas from a hodgepodge of hate groups. They espoused the philosophy of the Christian Identity religion, but adopted the style of the Nazi skin-

Tom Metzger (left), founder of the White Aryan Resistance, marches with members of the Ku Klux Klan. Many hate groups are interconnected and share ideologies.

heads. Many hate groups are interconnected.

In February 1997 a high-profile case again cast the spotlight on racist skinheads. James Burmeister, a 21-year-old white U.S. Army paratrooper, was convicted of shooting a black couple simply to earn a skinhead tattoo. The victims—Jackie Burden, 27, and Michael James, 36—were strolling down a street in Fayetteville,

North Carolina, when Burmeister struck.

During the trial, the jury was told that Burmeister and two other paratroopers had set out to beat blacks after drinking at a bar. Burmeister had talked about earning a spider's web tattoo, which could be achieved by killing a black person. Fellow paratrooper Randy Meadows testified that before leaving the bar, Burmeister had tucked a pistol under his belt.

Burmeister, from Thompson, Pennsylvania, was among 21 neo-Nazis at the Fort Bragg military base. The racist soldiers sang skinhead songs and even saluted a Nazi flag in their barracks.

Burmeister was convicted in the killings and is now serving two concurrent life sentences. His case focused worldwide attention on racism in the military and prompted the army to investigate the problem within its own ranks. In a worldwide probe, army officials found that fewer than 100 of the 7,600 soldiers investigated had links to white-supremacist groups.

Skinheads are a relatively new phenomenon. They burst onto the scene in England in the 1970s. At the time, however, the movement of rebellious kids was more about punk fashion than racism. But there was a subset of racists called the Nazi skinheads who terrorized nonwhites, preying on England's immigrants. Both brands of skinheads came to America in the mid-1980s. With their trademark shaved heads, bomber jackets, and Doc Marten boots, the Nazi skinheads stood out.

Bands of these racists have attacked blacks, Jews, gays, and other minorities. In the last decade, skinheads have been blamed for as many as 41 murders in the United States. Twenty-two of the victims whose deaths are attributed to skinhead attacks have been identified as members of racial minorities or as homosexuals, according to figures compiled by the Anti-Defamation League of B'nai B'rith, which monitors extremist groups.

The Anti-Defamation League said that racist skin-

Aryan Nations leader Richard Butler, photographed in his "church" on the grounds of the group's Hayden Lake, Idaho, compound. In the early 1990s Butler sought to rejuvenate his organization by recruiting violent young skinheads.

heads also have been responsible for thousands of assaults, firebombings, and desecrations of synagogues and cemeteries. The group put the number of skinheads at about 3,300, scattered across 40 states.

Between 1987 and 1994, skinheads were convicted of 33 murders throughout the country.

Their vicious attacks, fiery rhetoric, and menacing appearances landed them on television talk shows such as *Oprah* and *Geraldo*. Although their hatemongering appalled many Americans, it piqued the interest of aging hate-group leaders, who saw in the young and violent skinheads a chance to restock their waning memberships.

In the late 1980s, Tom Metzger, founder of the White Aryan Resistance (WAR), set his sights on recruiting skinheads to his movement. Metzger published a racist newspaper titled *WAR!*, sold instructional videotapes to racists around the country, and even put together his own cable access show, called *Race and Reason*. He saw in the skinheads a potential army of street fighters. With his 24-hour telephone hot line, Metzger encouraged listeners to use baseball bats "on the enemy." *WAR!* articles urged followers to "bash" nonwhites.

The California-based leader of WAR sent a representative to Portland, Oregon, to train skinheads to attack blacks and Jews. A jury later found that Metzger's leadership led to the death of Mulugeta Seraw. At the time of the Seraw murder, the skinhead movement had reached its peak. In 1991 the number of skinhead organizations totaled 144.

Other leaders of hate groups followed Metzger's example and tried to woo the skinheads. The Klan, Idaho's Aryan Nations, and the Church of the Creator opened their arms to the young racists. Former WAR representative and skinhead Dave Mazzella explained what made skinheads so appealing to the established racists.

"The old guys, they were a buncha bench sitters. The skinheads took it to the streets. It was a new resource to rejuvenate these organizations," he said.

That logic didn't escape Richard Butler, leader of the Aryan Nations. In 1990 he, too, wanted to rally the young racists, and Metzger helped him organize the skinheads. The biggest attraction turned out to be an annual youth festival, sponsored by Butler, that featured racist skinhead bands. Every year skinheads gather at Butler's compound in Hayden Lake, Idaho, to attend the concert.

The Aryan Nations once had a reputation as the most violent neo-Nazi group in America. In the mid-1970s, it ruled the white-supremacist world. Advocating a "whites only" homeland in the Pacific Northwest, the Aryan Nations prepared its members for a "white power" revolution.

Its leader, Butler, had been a follower of the Christian Identity and preached the faith from the Aryan Nations compound. His greatest achievement was being able to unify forces on the extreme right, and his group became an umbrella organization for a wide range of haters, including Klansmen, neo-Nazis, and Christian Identity believers.

But the military-style community collapsed in the 1980s after some of its members formed a terrorist underground army called the Order, which became one of the most dangerous right-wing groups since the Ku Klux Klan. The Order's mission was to terrorize the U.S. government. To that end, it adopted the structure of an army, built an arsenal of weapons, and even started a financial system to pay salaries to its soldiers. The Order bought land in the Idaho forest and used it as a military boot camp.

Robert Mathews, the group's leader, was inspired to form his underground army after reading a book called *The Turner Diaries*. Written by William Pierce, the work of fiction has become the bible of the militant racist movement. It's the story of a group of white supremacists who launch a full-scale race war. They commit acts of terror against a Jewish-controlled government, which eventually leads to the detonation of a nuclear bomb in the Pentagon.

Fashioning his group after the fictionalized one, Mathews took his trained members on a bloody crime spree that began in 1983. They killed a state trooper and in 1984 assassinated Alan Berg, a Denver-based

Scenes from Waco, Texas, 1993. This page: Carrying an automatic rifle, an ATF agent prepares to take up position in the early days of the law enforcement siege of the Branch Davidian compound. Facing page: After 51 days, the siege ends with a deadly conflagration. Waco and Ruby Ridge, Idaho, the site of an earlier shoot-out involving federal officials, became rallying cries for antigovernment militia organizations.

Jewish radio talk show host who had railed against their cause; they bombed synagogues. To finance their operations and collect the money that would be needed to establish a white homeland, the Order committed a series of armored car robberies and hauled in more than $4 million in a counterfeiting ring. The 18-month wave of terror came to an end when Mathews was killed in a shoot-out with federal agents and 24 members of the group were arrested.

The arrests dealt a serious blow to the Aryan Nations, and the group floundered for nearly a decade. In 1994 and 1995 Butler revived the Aryan Nations, thanks largely to the young racists who flocked to his movement. He also began using the media to spread his message of hate. Interviews with him began appearing in newspapers and magazines. His agents scoured the country signing up members of other racist groups, such as the White Order Knights in Colorado and the White Knights of Missouri.

The Aryan Nations received another shot in the arm in 1994, when it joined forces with a worldwide Hitler-worshiping group called Nebraska National Socialist German Workers Party–Overseas Organization. The neo-Nazi group has been banned in Germany since the late 1970s, when the German government outlawed the Nazi Party and its symbols. But it reaches people around the world through a tabloid it publishes in German, Dutch, French, Hungarian, Swedish, Danish, and English. The widely circulated propaganda is read by thousands of neo-Nazi skinheads in the United States.

As the Aryan Nations' strength returned, the skinhead movement started to wane. By 1994 the number

of skinhead groups had fallen to 34. Klanwatch has speculated that hate is not going away, but many of its adherents have outgrown the violent, radical sect and have joined other groups.

Today, with groups in 18 states, the Aryan Nations is the fastest-growing hate group, according to Klanwatch. Floyd Cochran, a former national spokesman for the Aryan Nations who defected in 1992, toured the country and revealed the inner workings of the hate groups. His job, he told a newspaper, had been to recruit teenagers, especially those who were emotionally disturbed.

But Cochran had a change of heart when his ex-wife told him that their son needed an operation to repair his cleft palate. He knew that if the Aryan Nations ever came to power, they would—as Hitler's Nazis had advocated during their reign in Germany—kill anyone who, like his son, had a genetic defect.

"It clicked something in me," Cochran told a union convention in Pennsylvania. "How do I say that was wrong about my son but it was all right for me to basically say the very same thing about people who are just born different from myself?"

The most recent phenomenon in the world of far-right extremism is the rise of militias, some of which are believed to have ties to racist organizations. Militias sprang into the national spotlight when a truck bomb leveled the Alfred P. Murrah Federal Building in Oklahoma City on the morning of April 19, 1995. Although federal investigators ultimately found no evidence linking the bombing to any militia, suspicion had initially fallen upon these groups, which were producing a stream of antigovernment invective. Timothy McVeigh was convicted of the bombing and sentenced to death in June 1997; his accomplice, Terry Nichols, received a life sentence the following year. Though the men weren't members of any militia group, they may have been inspired by militia ideology.

Numerous militia groups exist, and their beliefs vary. The most common thread, however, is suspicion and resentment of the federal government. Many militia members suspect federal officials of planning to establish a "world government" under the auspices of the United Nations. To facilitate this, they believe, the government is attempting to disarm its citizens. For this reason, militias zealously—some would say obsessively—oppose any restrictions on the Second Amendment right to bear arms. They stockpile weapons and train for the day they will have to defend themselves against the government.

Exactly two years after the Waco disaster, a truck bomb destroyed the Alfred P. Murrah Federal Building in Oklahoma City. Were the bombers motivated by militia rhetoric? Many Americans think so.

Though a majority of Americans might find these beliefs extreme, that doesn't mean that all militias qualify as hate groups; some, in fact, claim to be nonracial. But some of the extreme wings of the movement are fueled by racism. Klanwatch reports that some militias have ties to neo-Nazi and white-supremacist groups. And organizations that track militias claim that these groups have simply toned down their racist rhetoric in order to attract more members.

Militia groups point to two bloody confrontations as evidence that the U.S. government is repressive, violent, and untrustworthy. The two incidents galvanized the militia movement and led to an increase in membership.

The first occurred in 1992, when federal law enforcement officials attempted to arrest white-separatist Randy Weaver at his cabin in Ruby Ridge, Idaho, for failure to appear in court on a weapons charge. A gun battle and siege left Weaver's wife, his 14-year-old son, and a U.S. marshal dead. Many people in the militia movement considered the deaths of Weaver's wife and son inexcusable examples of the government's vindictiveness.

The second incident took place a year later. Agents of the federal Bureau of Alcohol, Tobacco, and Firearms (ATF) attempted a surprise raid on the compound of a religious cult near Waco, Texas, to serve a warrant on its leader, David Koresh, for weapons violations. But the cult members, known as Branch Davidians, were expecting the raid, and in a fierce gun battle they killed four ATF agents. There followed a 51-day standoff, during which the FBI surrounded the compound and attempted, unsuccessfully, to negotiate the Davidians' surrender. Finally, the decision was made to end the impasse by using modified tanks to batter through walls in the Davidians' main building and pump in tear gas. But the cult members weren't flushed out. Instead, fire swept through the building, killing 75 Davidians, including 17 children. In the aftermath of this tragedy, many militia members refused to accept the government's version of events: that the Davidians had started the fire in a mass suicide. Instead, they saw another bloody example of government tyranny.

Many militias subscribe to a theory of "leaderless resistance" that was laid out by Louis Beam, the Aryan Nations' "ambassador-at-large." According to the leaderless-resistance doctrine, instead of following orders issued by a leader, each member is part of a self-governed cell of six to eight men. Members of a cell stay informed about events through militia newspapers, leaflets, or the Internet. They plan the course of action they deem appropriate. That way, if an individual or even an entire cell is arrested for a terrorist crime, the government cannot hold the larger group responsible.

Membership in every hate group waxes and wanes. And though these groups have been directly responsible for scores of vicious acts of hate, they have influenced countless others. How the nation can most effectively combat crimes motivated by hate is a question that has yet to be fully answered.

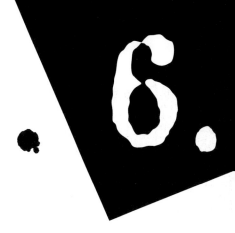

PUNISHING HATE

The shocking rise in hate crimes has triggered a nationwide movement in favor of boosting penalties for crimes inspired by bias. And many legislatures have, in fact, heeded the public's call, enacting laws that enhance punishment for those convicted of targeting a victim based on hostility toward the victim's race, ethnicity, religion, gender, or sexual orientation. But these anti-hate-crime laws have raised thorny constitutional questions. At the heart of the matter is whether and under what circumstances crimes inspired by hate can be singled out for increased punishment without abridging the First Amendment right of freedom of speech.

The debate over whether all speech should be free

A black family that moves into a predominantly white neighborhood may be greeted with racial slurs, graffiti, or vandalism. Whether and how such racially motivated intimidation may be punished has been at issue in several recent court cases.

and whether laws can regulate hate has divided civil rights and civil liberties groups. Lawyers, courts, and legislatures have argued over how to separate words that carry ideas from words that actually hurt. Two pivotal cases that have gone all the way to the U.S. Supreme Court—*R.A.V. v. the City of St. Paul* and *State of Wisconsin v. Todd Mitchell*—have helped set the parameters of hate-crimes legislation.

In St. Paul, Minnesota, Russ and Laura Jones found their dream home: a large, four-bedroom house with a fenced-in yard where their five children could play. The delighted family moved into the home in March 1990. But Russ and Laura Jones were not only homeowners but also pioneers: they were the first black family to move into the working-class block.

Two weeks after they had settled in, someone slashed the tires of their family car. A few weeks later, a car window was smashed in. Then one day, passing skinheads yelled "nigger" at the Joneses' nine-year-old son.

But the most menacing incident occurred in the early morning of June 21, 1990. Startled awake by voices and footsteps outside his house, Russ Jones darted to the bedroom window and beheld a terrifying sight. There, in the middle of his yard, was a burning cross. The fiery symbol of racial hatred ignited fear in the Joneses' hearts.

The message was loud and clear: the entire Jones family was vulnerable to the forces of hate. Russ Jones spelled it out for his wife: "We are being told we had better get out of here or something bad is going to happen."

The cross that burned in the Joneses' yard and the arrest that followed sparked a heated debate about hate-crime laws, which prescribe more-severe penalties for crimes motivated by bias than for similar crimes committed without such motivation. The incident led to a landmark Supreme Court decision that would have ramifications in every state in the country.

A young man burns the American flag during a demonstration in Washington, D.C. In 1990 the Supreme Court ruled flag burning a form of expression protected by the First Amendment. When skinhead Robert Viktora was charged with violating an anti-hate-speech ordinance in St. Paul, Minnesota, for burning a cross on the lawn of a black family, his lawyer pointed to that decision in arguing that cross burning, too, was constitutionally protected.

Police arrested Robert Viktora, a 17-year-old high school dropout and skinhead. He and his friends had made the cross by taping together chair legs. They carried their crudely made construction into the Joneses' fenced-in yard and torched it.

After the arrest was made, prosecutors had to decide how the offender would be charged. Options included charging Viktora with arson or trespassing, but they chose instead to charge him with breaking St. Paul's

"Let there be no mistake about our belief that burning a cross in someone's front yard is reprehensible," wrote Justice Antonin Scalia (above) in the Supreme Court's 1992 R.A.V. decision, which overturned St. Paul's hate-speech law. "But St. Paul has sufficient means at its disposal to prevent such behavior without adding the First Amendment to the fire."

new "hate-speech" ordinance. The measure outlawed any symbol, such as burning crosses and Nazi swastikas, that might "arouse anger, alarm or resentment in others on the basis of race, color, creed, religion, or gender."

Viktora's lawyer, Ed Cleary, agreed that his client's act was loathsome and deserved punishment. But Cleary argued that the St. Paul ordinance was unconstitutional because it violated Viktora's right to free speech. A cross burning and other symbols, no matter how hateful, are forms of expression, he said. As such they are protected under the First Amendment, Cleary argued.

"In a country that values free speech, we should not have a law that says expressing certain ideas, however offensive they may be, is in itself a crime," Cleary told a reporter.

He pointed to an earlier ruling of the Supreme Court that supported his case. In 1990 the Court had ruled flag burning a protected form of expression. Someone who burns the American flag may be punished under a law against outdoor fires but can't be punished under a law against dishonoring the flag. That law would be punishing the content of the flag burner's expression, not the act itself.

Cleary won the case in Ramsey County juvenile court. The judge agreed that cross burning was a form of protected speech and also said that the law was too broad because it could apply to any act that made someone angry. The court, applying its mandate to enforce the Constitution, struck down St. Paul's hate-speech ordinance and was then compelled to dismiss the case against Viktora.

The legal battle over Viktora's conduct, however, was far from over. St. Paul appealed the case to the Minnesota Supreme Court, which ruled in the city's favor. The judges on that court declared the ordinance valid. Cross burning could be banned, they said, because it was a form of "fighting words." Fighting words—expressions that are likely to provoke violence—don't merit the full protection of the First Amendment, as the Supreme Court ruled in 1942 in the case of *Chaplinsky v. New Hampshire*. In that case, the defendant was accused of inciting a riot in Rochester, New Hampshire, by calling a policeman "a goddammed racketeer" and "a damned fascist" and saying that "the whole government of Rochester are fascists or agents of fascists." In his opinion, Supreme Court justice Frank Murphy stated:

> There are certain well-defined and narrowly limited classes of speech, the prevention and punishment of which have never been thought to raise any Constitutional problem. These include . . . "fighting" words—those which by their very utterance inflict injury or tend to incite an immediate breach of the peace. It has been well observed that such utterances are no essential part of any exposition of ideas, and are of such slight social value . . . that any benefit that may be derived from them is clearly outweighed by the social interest in order. . . .

Despite this precedent, Cleary took Viktora's case to the U.S. Supreme Court, which has ultimate authority to interpret the Constitution. In a stunning decision rendered on June 22, 1992, the Supreme Court sided with Cleary, voting unanimously to strike down the St. Paul ordinance in the historic case known as *R.A.V.*

The Court, in an opinion written by Justice Antonin Scalia, ruled that the ordinance was unconstitutional because it violated the First Amendment's protection of free speech. But the justices sharply disagreed in explaining how they arrived at the decision. Five justices agreed that the ordinance was unconstitutional because it could be used only to punish fighting words that applied to race, color, creed, or religion and not fighting words that applied to other categories. For example, the law could be used to punish Viktora for expressing racial hatred, but not to punish someone who expressed hatred of dropout skinheads like Viktora. In their ruling, the justices said lawmakers cannot single out for punishment certain kinds of hatred.

In his opinion, Scalia noted that St. Paul didn't need a special law to punish Viktora, who could have been punished under other laws that ban terrorist threats, arson, or criminal damage to property. Conviction for any one of those acts could have put him away for a prison term.

"Let there be no mistake about our belief that burning a cross in someone's front yard is reprehensible," Scalia wrote. "But St. Paul has sufficient means at its disposal to prevent such behavior without adding the First Amendment to the fire."

Four other justices agreed that the ordinance was too broad, but disagreed with Scalia's reasoning. They said racist speech *should* carry special penalties. "Conduct that creates special risks or causes special harms may be prohibited by special rules," wrote Justice John Paul Stevens.

> Lighting a fire near an ammunition dump or a gasoline storage tank is especially dangerous; such behavior may be punished more severely than burning trash in a vacant lot. Threatening someone because of her race or religious beliefs may cause particularly severe trauma or touch off a riot . . . and may be punished more severely than threats against someone based on, say, his support of a particular athletic team.

Reaction to the Court's *R.A.V.* decision varied. Civil libertarians applauded it because of their belief that punishing speech, even hateful speech, violates the First Amendment, which protects speech that may be found offensive by the majority. And, civil libertarians pointed out, it's hard to know someone's motive, even in a hate crime. Trying to get into a defendant's head comes dangerously close to mind control, they argued.

Ed Cleary, Viktora's defense attorney, had said that his client knew he was committing an insensitive prank but didn't intend to intimidate the Jones family. Cleary told the press: "We do such a poor job of teaching history—especially black history—in this country that it isn't that surprising that some white suburban kids wouldn't realize the significance of what happened here."

Civil rights groups, on the other hand, were distressed by the *R.A.V.* decision. They said that not all speech should be free, especially speech that is used as terrorism, designed to threaten and intimidate an entire community. Burning a pile of garbage in someone's yard and lighting a cross may both constitute arson, but these acts are very different in nature. Hate speech such as that committed by Viktora, civil rights groups argued, deserves added punishment. And, they asked, what about the Joneses' constitutional right to live where they chose?

Less than 24 hours after the U.S. Supreme Court delivered its *R.A.V.* ruling, a state supreme court would issue a ruling in another hate-crime case. That case, involving an attack on a white boy by black teenagers, would spark further debate about how the nation can fight bigotry without stomping on the right to free speech. Ultimately, the case would help define the nation's legal response to bias crimes.

PILING ON
PUNISHMENT

odd Mitchell gathered with a group of friends outside an apartment complex in Kenosha, Wisconsin, in October 1989. The group of young black men were talking about the film *Mississippi Burning*, which contained racially charged themes. The movie, based on a historical incident that occurred in 1964, is about the murder of three civil rights workers in the South and the ensuing federal investigation into their disappearances. The men were particularly angered by one scene, in which a member of the Ku Klux Klan severely beats a black boy who is praying.

Mitchell, who had not seen the movie, was listening to the others describe it in disturbing detail. Then he asked the group: "Do you all feel hyped up to move on some white people? There goes a white boy. Go get him."

He pointed to Gregory Reddick, a 14-year-old who was crossing the street on his way home. That night in October, Mitchell stood in the parking lot while eight of his friends viciously attacked Reddick. They stole the boy's leather high-top sneakers, then beat him senseless. The attack sent Reddick into a coma for four days and caused permanent head injuries.

Mitchell, 19 years old at the time, flagged down police to help Reddick after the attack. Although he didn't participate in the beating, he was later charged with inciting his friends to attack the boy. His alleged motive was racial: he had urged his friends to attack the white teen to exact revenge for past abuses endured by blacks.

Because he was accused of having singled out a victim solely on the basis of race, Mitchell was charged under Wisconsin's hate-crime law. The law allows extra punishment when a victim is chosen for reasons of "race, religion, color, disability, sexual orientation, national origin or ancestry."

Mitchell was slapped with a four-year jail sentence: two years for his part in the attack, plus two more years for picking Reddick because he was white.

Mitchell's lawyer said that the punishment that had been piled on because Mitchell had goaded his friends had violated his client's right to free speech. He appealed to the Wisconsin State Supreme Court.

In a 5-2 vote, that court agreed with Mitchell's attorney, overturning part of Mitchell's conviction and reducing his sentence. The court said nobody has a right to participate in an attack and that Mitchell should be punished for the crime. But it also ruled that Mitchell should not be punished for his words because everyone has a right to his or her beliefs.

The court threw out the state's hate-crime law. The justices said that the law went too far, punishing offensive *thought*. In their decision, they declared that "the Wisconsin legislature cannot criminalize bigoted thought with which it disagrees."

Once again, however, the legal fight was far from over. Wisconsin attorney general James Doyle took the

Mitchell case to the U.S. Supreme Court, which agreed to hear it.

Much was at stake. Many states had laws that, like the Wisconsin statute, boosted sentences for crimes of hate. If the Supreme Court agreed with the Wisconsin State Supreme Court in striking down Wisconsin's hate-crime law, every other such state law would be invalid.

As is typical in high-profile cases, groups on both sides of the enhanced-sentencing issue pitched their views in the court of public opinion before the lawyers argued the case in front of the Supreme Court justices. At the forefront of the fight for maintaining hate-crime laws was the Anti-Defamation League. Jess Hordes, a spokesman for the league, told a reporter, "Society has a right to treat certain conduct with greater concern. Crimes of hate tear at the fragile

A Klansman prepares to beat a praying African-American boy in a scene from the 1988 motion picture Mississippi Burning. *It was this scene in particular that had enraged the black youths who attacked Gregory Reddick.*

"A physical assault is not by any stretch of the imagination expressive conduct protected by the First Amendment," declared Chief Justice William Rehnquist (above) in the U.S. Supreme Court's unanimous State of Wisconsin v. Todd Mitchell *decision. The ruling cleared the way for statutes that impose extra penalties for hate crimes.*

bonds that hold together America's diverse society."

People on the other side of the issue felt just as strongly that hate-crime laws were a threat to individual liberties. "If government can punish racist thought today," declared Susan Gellman, a lawyer for Mitchell, "then tomorrow they can punish unpatriotic or antiwar thought."

Seven prominent constitutional-law specialists also expressed their opposition to the hate law in amicus curiae, or "friend of the court," briefs—written arguments submitted to the Supreme Court by experts not involved directly in the case being considered. "As dangerous and offensive as any expression of racism or bigotry may be, considerably more dangerous is any attempt by the government to control the minds of its citizens," warned Northwestern University law professor Martin Redish in one such brief.

After reading the amicus curiae briefs and hearing oral arguments from both sides, the Supreme Court weighed the constitutional issues involved in the case called *State of Wisconsin v. Todd Mitchell.* On June 11, 1994, the Court announced its unanimous opinion: the Wisconsin hate-crime law passed constitutional muster. Rejecting the assertion that the law violated the First Amendment guarantees of free speech, the justices declared that the law was valid because it punished conduct, not thoughts or words. The justices spelled out the major difference between *State of Wisconsin v. Todd Mitchell* and *R.A.V.*, which the Court had decided earlier. Burning a cross or displaying any symbol is an expression of free speech, they said. Beating someone is not.

"Whereas the ordinance struck down in *R.A.V.* was

explicitly directed at expression . . . the statute, in this case, is aimed at conduct unprotected by the First Amendment," wrote Chief Justice William Rehnquist. "A physical assault is not by any stretch of the imagination expressive conduct protected by the First Amendment," the chief justice added.

The Supreme Court's decision cleared the way for the states and the federal government to impose increased prison sentences on assailants convicted of hate crimes, a strategy civil rights groups believe holds the greatest promise for combating crimes of bias.

Others aren't so optimistic. Not only do hate-crime laws endanger free-speech rights, critics charge, but they could also wind up hurting the very groups they are most intended to protect. These critics speculate that the laws will be used more often against minorities—that more blacks will go to jail for black-on-white crimes than whites for the more commonly committed white-on-black crimes.

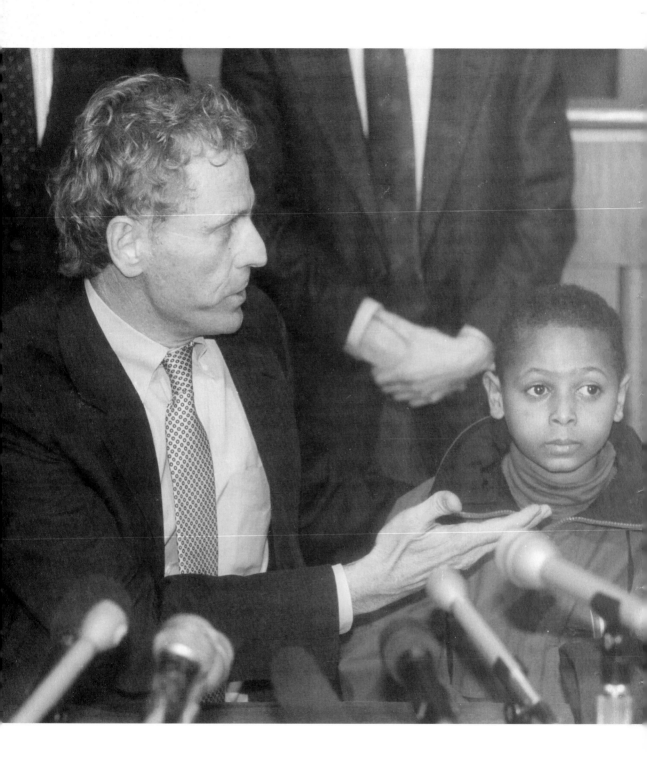

8.

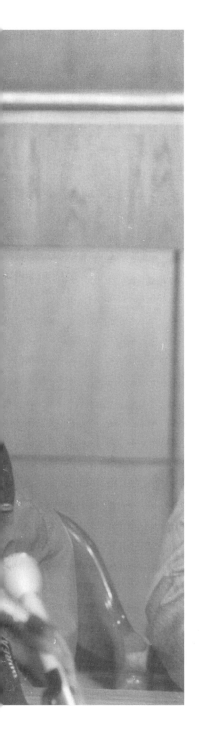

FIGHTING HATE

Almost every state has laws that stiffen the punishment for people convicted of hate crimes. When hate groups are behind those crimes, criminal courts aren't the only places where justice is meted out. Victims can seek recompense in civil courts as well. There, leaders of hate groups don't face jail time. They face bankruptcy and the possible destruction of their organizations.

Morris Dees, a well-known civil rights attorney from Alabama, pioneered this strategy. He cofounded an agency to advance the legal rights of the poor, the

Though their hatemongering may incite followers to violence, leaders of hate groups rarely face prosecution. But attorney Morris Dees (left) showed that this doesn't make them untouchable. Dees pioneered the use of civil suits to hold hate groups and leaders financially accountable for crimes they inspire. Here Dees gestures toward Henok Seraw at a news conference following a multimillion-dollar award against the White Aryan Resistance and two of its leaders in the murder of the boy's father, Mulugeta.

Tom Metzger, leader of the White Aryan Resistance, at a news conference after a jury in Portland found him and his son John liable in the death of Mulugeta Seraw. "Dr. Caligari's box," Metzger declared, referring to a famous 1919 horror film, "is open and I can advocate violence now."

Southern Poverty Law Center. Largely as the result of his efforts, the center has gained a national reputation for its efforts to fight hate groups.

Dees has won big cash judgments against white-supremacist groups by convincing juries that racist leaders can be held responsible for the tragic consequences of their hatemongering. In 1987 he first used this technique after a young black man, Michael Donald, was abducted and hanged from a tree in Mobile, Alabama. One member of the Klan had been convicted in the lynching and another had pleaded guilty. "We didn't know him," said one of the Klansmen. "We just wanted to show the Klan strength in Alabama."

Dees filed a lawsuit on behalf of Donald's mother against the United Klans of America. Using secret documents, he showed how the Klan's promotion of racial violence incited Donald's killers.

In a stunning verdict, the jury sided with the Donald family, awarding $7 million to Mrs. Donald. Unable to come up with the money, the Klan was forced to turn over its national headquarters to her. She later sold the building.

The next year, Dees went to court on behalf of Mulugeta Seraw, the Ethiopian immigrant who was beaten to death by skinheads in Portland. Convinced that the trail of blood led to Tom Metzger, head of the White Aryan Resistance, and his son John Metzger, Dees battled them in civil court. He set out to prove to a jury that the Metzgers encouraged the skinheads to kill victims like Seraw.

The Metzgers represented themselves in court. A former Grand Dragon of the Ku Klux Klan, Tom Metzger was the most prominent white supremacist in the country. He had recruited white youths as skinheads in about 100 U.S. cities. As the head of WAR's skinhead faction, 22-year-old John Metzger had influence with the growing number of young racists.

The WAR philosophy was violent, racist, and anti-Semitic. The Metzgers' vision of an ideal America included pushing out all Latinos and Asians and creating separate states for white and black people.

Dees' case pivoted on a single key witness, Dave Mazzella, the former vice president of Metzger's neo-Nazi Aryan Youth Movement. He knew that putting Mazzella on the stand would be a risky maneuver. Volatile and aimless, Mazzella had found it hard to stay out of trouble with the law, and his credibility could be impugned. And Mazzella himself had reason to fear testifying: a previous leader of the Aryan Youth Movement was nailed to a cross by his fellow skinheads after he quit the organization.

Despite the obstacles, Mazzella turned out to be a compelling witness. He testified that the Metzgers had sent him to Portland on a mission: to train skinheads to attack blacks and Jews. He said Metzger had instructed him to teach young racists to provoke their victims before attacking them with baseball bats. By starting a fight, the skinheads were told, they could later claim they had acted in self-defense.

Tom Metzger said Mazzella was a liar. He denied instructing him to organize and train skinheads. He claimed the Seraw murder was simply a street fight that had turned deadly.

The Multnomah County Circuit Court jury, made up of 10 whites, a Japanese-American, and a Hawaiian, deliberated about five hours before reaching the verdict. In an 11-1 vote, they found the Metzgers liable. (Unlike a typical criminal verdict, in which all the jurors must agree, civil verdicts in Oregon require agreement by only 9 of the 12 jurors.)

Tom Metzger was ordered to pay $5 million; his son John, $1 million; and WAR, $3 million—all in damages to the family of Seraw. Ken Mieske and Kyle Brewster were ordered to pay $500,000 each.

After the verdict was announced, Seraw's father, Tekuneh, said through a translator, "They have avenged my son's death for me. This is the happiest I have felt since my son died. I am happy for the system."

Dees said the verdict clearly drew a line between free speech and conduct. "This jury has spoken loud and clear that in this country, the First Amendment guarantees the right to hate people and say whatever you want. But it does not give you the right to hurt people."

If the trial served notice on the leaders of America's hate groups that they could no longer hide behind the actions of the unstable people they incited to violence, in many ways it also constituted a wake-up call for the rest of the nation. The face of violent racism, it became apparent, had changed from the days of white hoods

Ironies of intolerance: A black woman shields a white man, presumably a Ku Klux Klan sympathizer, who was being beaten with sticks by demonstrators protesting a Klan rally in Ann Arbor, Michigan.

and burning crosses. Today's racists aren't so easy to identify; they're just as likely to wear suits and carry briefcases.

A defiant Tom Metzger vowed to continue to publish his racist newspaper and to tape his TV program, *Race and Reason.* "We're going out and celebrate tonight," Metzger said after the verdict was announced.

> The white separatist movement won't be stopped in a
> puny town like Portland. We're too deep. We're imbed-
> ded now. Don't you understand? We're in your colleges,
> we're in your armies, we're in your police forces, we're in
> your technical areas, we're in your banks. Where do you
> think a lot of these skinheads disappeared to? . . . We've
> planted the seeds. Stopping Tom Metzger is not gonna
> change what's going to happen in this country.

No one in America can close his or her eyes to crimes of bias. Their terrible toll is felt in every area of the country, in homes and in schools, in places of worship and on streets, in the minds of those who have been intimidated and the hearts of those who have lost a loved one.

Some observers believe that the legal system provides the best weapon for combating the nation's epidemic of hate crimes. Tough laws that stiffen criminal penalties for bias-motivated offenses, they argue, not only deter hatemongers from committing their crimes out of fear of the consequences but also, by expressing the moral outrage of the community, send a strong message that bias itself is unacceptable.

But others say that legislative measures haven't stamped out bias crimes and never will because what gives rise to these acts—prejudice and hatred—are in the mind, beyond the reach of the law. In fact, laws that try to control thoughts—even ugly, hateful thoughts—are themselves illegal. And by the time a hate-crime case arrives in court, the damage has already been done: an innocent person has been harassed, hurt, or worse.

A more effective solution would be to change the attitudes that give rise to hate crimes. Thus, some people maintain, we should be fighting hate crime not so much in the courtroom as in the classroom. If children could be taught tolerance of others, they would be less susceptible to the forces of hatred and prejudice. However, given the all-too-apparent limitations of America's educational system, no rational observer would suggest that the schools alone might eradicate bigotry—any more than the courts alone might accomplish this.

The question of how the nation should respond to hate crimes remains very much unanswered, and the issue goes to the heart of who we are as a people. Two fundamental American values—individual liberty and social justice—frame the debate. On the one hand, we insist that everyone has the right to his or her beliefs, along with the right to express those beliefs, regardless of how offensive they might be to other members of society. On the other hand, words, symbols, and images can hurt and intimidate, and verbal and symbolic expressions of hate, which are legal, often lead to physical expressions, which are not. So a crucial challenge remains: How can we promote equality for all if we allow some to spout a bitter stream of hurtful invective? How can we separate expression and action, especially when the two are so dangerously close?

Further Reading

Chalmers, David M. *Hooded Americanism: The History of the Ku Klux Klan*. Durham, N.C.: Duke University Press, 1987.

Dees, Morris, and Steve Fiffer. *Hate on Trial: The Case Against America's Most Dangerous Neo Nazi*. New York: Villard Books, 1993.

Ezekiel, Raphael. *The Racist Mind: Portraits of American Neo Nazis and Klansmen*. New York: Penguin Books, 1995.

Flynn, Kevin, and Gary Gerhardt. *The Silent Brotherhood*. New York: The Free Press, 1995.

Levin, Jack, and Jack McDevitt. *Hate Crimes: The Rising Tide of Bigotry and Bloodshed*. New York: Plenum Press, 1993.

Ridgeway, James. *Blood in the Face: The Ku Klux Klan, Aryan Nations, Nazi Skinheads and the Rise of a New White Culture*. New York: Thunder's Mouth Press, 1990.

Stern, Kenneth S. *A Force upon the Plain: The American Militia Movement and the Politics of Hate*. Norman: University of Oklahoma Press, 1996.

Wade, Wyn Craig. *The Fiery Cross: The Ku Klux Klan in America*. New York: Simon & Schuster, 1987.

Winters, Paul. *Hate Crimes*. San Diego: Greenhaven Press, 1996.

Index

LAURA D'ANGELO is a freelance writer and editor living in New York City. She is also the author of *The FBI's Most Wanted* in Chelsea House's Crime, Justice, and Punishment series.

AUSTIN SARAT is William Nelson Cromwell Professor of Jurisprudence and Political Science at Amherst College, where he also chairs the Department of Law, Jurisprudence and Social Thought. Professor Sarat is the author or editor of 23 books and numerous scholarly articles. Among his books are *Law's Violence, Sitting in Judgment: Sentencing the White Collar Criminal*, and *Justice and Injustice in Law and Legal Theory*. He has received many academic awards and held several prestigious fellowships. In addition, he is a nationally recognized teacher and educator whose teaching has been featured in the *New York Times*, on the *Today* show, and on National Public Radio's *Fresh Air*.

Picture Credits